ISBNs:
978-1-967064-53-3 (paperback),
978-1-967064-54-0 (hardback),
978-1-967064-55-7 (kindle edition)

First Edition: December 2025 | Author: Lulu Pixo

This book belongs to:

_____

Table of Contents

Santa & Reindeer Extra Treats

Santa's Treats

Holiday Kid Favorite

Reindeer Treats

Classic Gingerbread Cookies

Adapted From: Mrs. Lincoln's Boston Cook Book, 1884

Prep Time: 15 minutes **Bake Time:** 8–10 minutes
Chill Time: 1 hour **Servings:** 24–30 cookies

Ingredients

- ½ cup butter
- ½ cup sugar
- ½ cup molasses
- 1 large egg
- 2½ cups flour
- 1 tsp baking soda
- 1 tsp ground ginger
- ½ tsp cinnamon
- ¼ tsp nutmeg
- Pinch of salt

Directions

1. **Cream the butter and sugar** until light and smooth.
2. **Beat in the egg and molasses** until fully blended.
3. In a separate bowl, mix together the **flour, baking soda, salt, and spices.**
4. Add dry ingredients to the molasses mixture; mix until a soft dough forms.
5. **Cover and chill for 1 hour.**
6. Roll dough ¼ inch thick on a lightly floured surface.
7. Cut into festive shapes.
8. Bake at **350°F for 8–10 minutes,** until edges are set.

Optional Variations:
- Add a simple vanilla icing after cookies cool.
- Press holiday sprinkles onto the dough before baking.
- For extra soft cookies, remove from oven at 8 minutes.

4

Old-Fashioned Sugar Cookies

Adapted From: The Boston Cooking-School Cook Book, 1896

Prep Time: 10 minutes
Chill Time: 30 minutes

Bake Time: 8–10 minutes
Servings: 24–30 cookies

Ingredients

- ½ cup butter
- 1 cup sugar
- 2 eggs
- 1 tsp vanilla extract
- 2 cups flour
- 1 tsp baking powder
- ¼ tsp salt

Directions

1. **Cream butter and sugar** until light and fluffy.
2. Beat in **eggs and vanilla.**
3. Combine **flour, baking powder, and salt;** stir into batter.
4. Chill dough **30 minutes** for easy rolling.
5. Roll out and cut shapes OR scoop dough and flatten slightly.
6. Bake at **350°F for 8–10** minutes.

Optional Variations:
- Sprinkle tops with colored sanding sugar before baking.
- Add ½ tsp almond extract for a festive twist.
- For soft cookies, bake until edges are just barely golden.
- Drizzle with sprinkles and icing for extra festive flare.

Molasses Crinkle Cookies

Adapted From: The Rumford Complete Cook Book, 1908

Prep Time: 10 minutes
Chill Time: None

Bake Time: 10–12 minutes
Servings: 24 cookies

Ingredients

- ½ cup butter
- 1 cup sugar
- 1 egg
- ¼ cup molasses
- 2 cups flour

- 1 tsp baking soda
- 1 tsp ginger
- ½ tsp cinnamon
- ¼ tsp cloves
- Pinch of salt

- Extra sugar for rolling

Directions

1. Cream **butter and sugar**.
2. Add **egg and molasses** and mix well.
3. Stir together **flour, baking soda, salt, and spices**.
4. Add dry mixture to the wet ingredients.
5. Roll dough into small balls and **coat generously in sugar.**
6. Bake at **350°F for 10–12 minutes,** until tops crack.

Optional Variations:
- Coat in coarse sparkling sugar for a holiday shine.
- For chewier cookies, remove from oven at first sign of cracks.
- Add ½ tsp orange zest for a warm Christmas aroma.

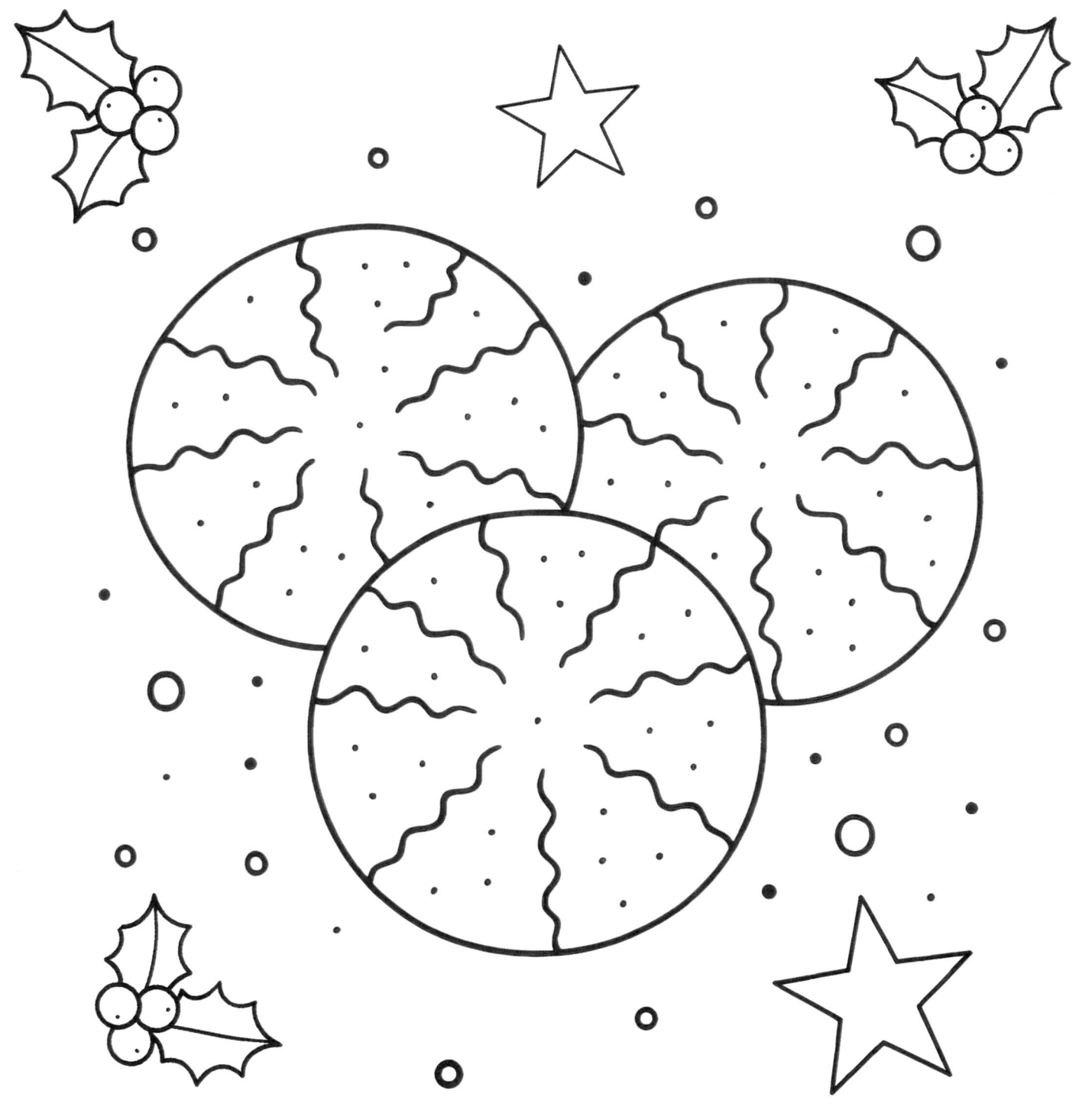

Peppermint Drop Cookies

Adapted From: The Neighborhood Cook Book, 1912

Prep Time: 10 minutes
Chill Time: None

Bake Time: 10–12 minutes
Servings: 24 cookies

Ingredients

- ½ cup butter
- 1 cup sugar
- 1 large egg
- ½ cup milk
- 2 cups flour
- ½ tsp baking soda
- ¼ tsp salt
- ½ tsp peppermint extract
- Optional: crushed peppermint candy or sprinkles

Directions

1. Cream **butter and sugar** until fluffy.
2. Add the **egg** and beat until smooth.
3. Stir in **milk and peppermint extract.**
4. In a separate bowl, combine **flour, baking soda, and salt.**
5. Add dry mixture to wet mixture until a soft dough forms.
6. Drop small spoonfuls onto a cookie sheet.
7. Bake at **350°F for 10–12** minutes, until edges are barely golden.

Optional Variations:
- After baking, sprinkle warm cookies with crushed peppermint candies.
- For "peppermint snow" cookies, dust with powdered sugar once cooled.
- Add a tiny swirl of red food coloring to the dough for a marbled effect.

Scottish Shortbread

Adapted From: The White House Cook Book, 1887

Prep Time: 10 minutes
Chill Time: None

Bake Time: 18–20 minutes
Servings: 16 bars or wedges

Ingredients

- 1 cup butter
- ½ cup sugar
- 2 cups flour
- Pinch of salt

Directions

1. Cream **butter and sugar** until smooth.
2. Add **flour and salt**; mix until crumbly and soft.
3. Press dough into an 8-inch pan OR roll ½ inch thick and shape.
4. Score lines with a knife and prick the top with a fork.
5. Bake at **325°F for 18–20** minutes, until very pale golden.

Optional Variations:
- Sprinkle lightly with extra sugar immediately after baking.
- Add ½ tsp almond extract or vanilla extract for deeper flavor.
- Dip cooled wedges in melted chocolate for a festive cookie tin treat.

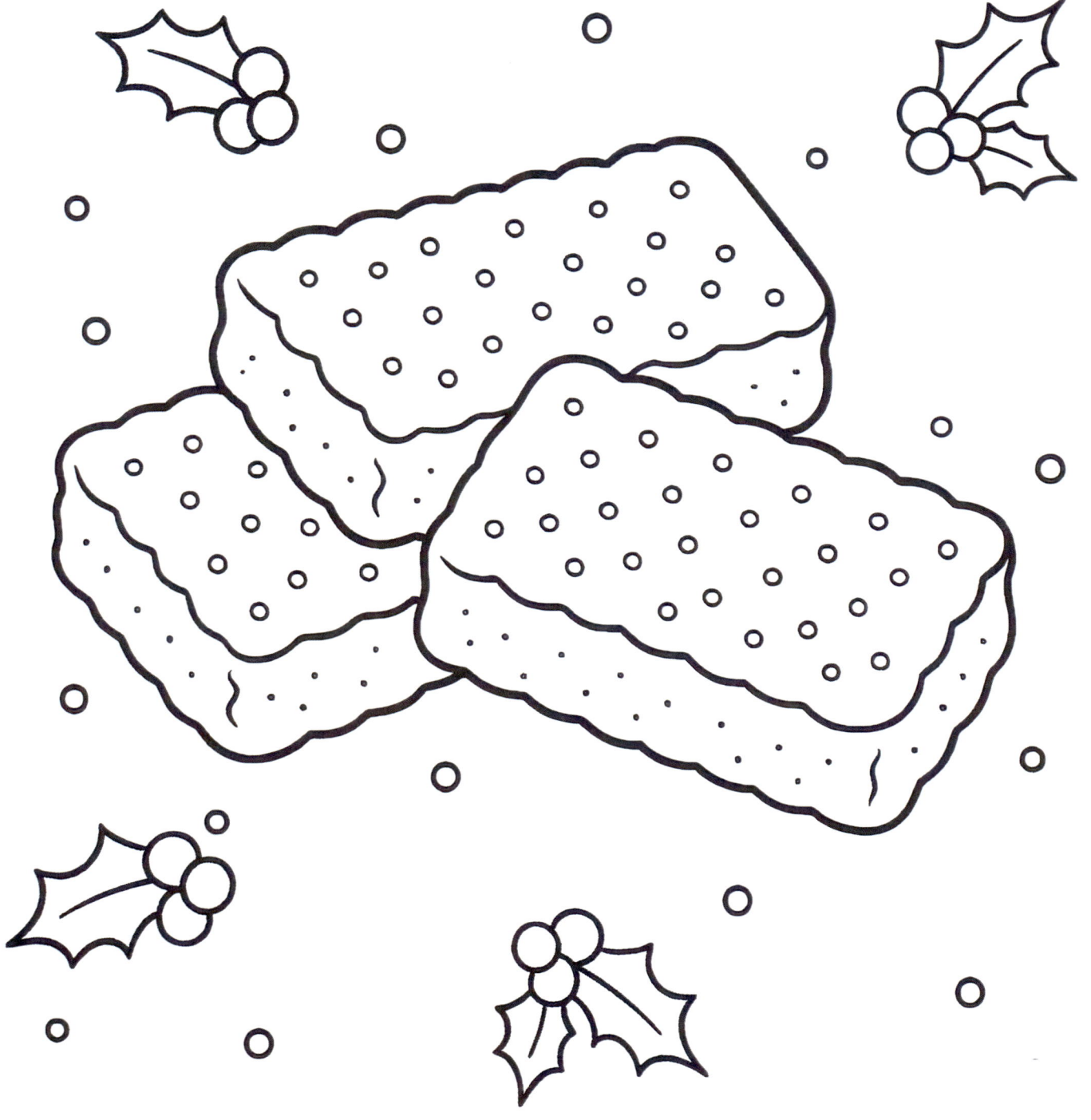

Cinnamon Stars (Zimtsterne)

Adapted From: German holiday classic

Prep Time: 10 minutes
Chill Time: None

Bake Time: 10–12 minutes
Servings: 24 cookies

Ingredients

- 2 large egg whites
- 1½ cups powdered sugar
- 2 cups finely ground almonds
- 1 tsp cinnamon
- ½ tsp vanilla
- Pinch of salt
- Extra powdered sugar for rolling

Directions

1. Beat egg whites until stiff peaks form.
2. Gently fold in powdered sugar, almonds, cinnamon, vanilla, and salt.
3. Mix into a soft, sticky dough.
4. Sprinkle a surface with powdered sugar and roll dough ¼ inch thick.
5. Cut out stars using a star-shaped cutter.
6. Place on lined baking sheet.
7. Bake at 325°F for 8–10 minutes, until edges are just set.
   a. (These cookies should stay soft and chewy.)

Optional Variations:
- Brush tops lightly with a thin layer of powdered-sugar glaze before baking.
- Add a pinch of nutmeg or ginger for a spiced Christmas twist.
- Top with white icing or glazed sugar and red sprinkles.

Victorian Fruit Drop Cookies

Adapted From: Victorian-era fruit drop cookies

Prep Time: 10 minutes
Chill Time: None

Bake Time: 10–12 minutes
Servings: About 24 cookies

Ingredients

- ½ cup butter
- 1 cup sugar
- 1 egg
- ½ cup milk
- 2 cups flour
- ½ tsp baking soda
- ¼ tsp salt
- ½ tsp cinnamon
- ¼ tsp nutmeg
- ½ cup finely chopped dried fruit (raisins, currants, or mixed fruit)

Directions

1. Cream **butter and sugar** until fluffy.
2. Beat in **egg** until smooth.
3. Stir in **milk**.
4. In a separate bowl, combine **flour, baking soda, salt, cinnamon, & nutmeg.**
5. Add dry ingredients to wet ingredients.
6. Fold in **chopped dried fruit.**
7. Drop spoonfuls of dough onto a baking sheet.
8. Bake at **350°F for 10–12 minutes** until lightly golden.

Optional Variations:

- Add ¼ cup chopped nuts for a traditional fruitcake flavor.
- Dust cooled cookies with powdered sugar for a Victorian holiday finish.
- Use dried cranberries for a bright Christmas twist.

Snickerdoodles

Adapted From: late-1800s American cookbooks

Prep Time: 10 minutes   **Bake Time:** 8–10 minutes
Chill Time: None   **Servings:** 24 cookies

Ingredients

Cookie Dough
- ½ cup butter
- 1 cup sugar
- 1 egg
- 1½ cups flour

- ½ tsp baking soda
- ¼ tsp salt

Cinnamon Sugar
- 2 tbsp sugar
- 1 tsp cinnamon

Directions

1. Cream **butter and sugar** until smooth.
2. Beat in the **egg.**
3. In a separate bowl, combine **flour, baking soda, and salt.**
4. Add dry ingredients to wet mixture; form soft dough.
5. Mix **cinnamon and sugar** in a small bowl.
6. Roll dough into balls and coat thoroughly in **cinnamon sugar.**
7. Bake at **350°F for 8–10 minutes,** until lightly cracked.

Optional Variations:
- Add ⅛ tsp nutmeg for a warmer Christmas spice.
- For thicker cookies, chill dough for 15–20 minutes.
- Roll in coarse sanding sugar for sparkle.

Lemon Snowflake Cookies

Adapted From: TThe Boston Cooking-School Cook Book, 1896

Prep Time: 10 minutes **Bake Time:** 10–12 minutes
Chill Time: None **Servings:** 24 cookies

Ingredients

- ½ cup butter
- 1 cup sugar
- 1 egg
- 1 tbsp lemon juice
- 1 tsp lemon zest
- 2 cups flour
- 1 tsp baking powder
- ¼ tsp salt
- Powdered sugar (for rolling)

Directions

1. Cream **butter and sugar** until light.
2. Add **egg, lemon juice, and lemon zest.**
3. In another bowl, whisk **flour, baking powder, and salt.**
4. Add dry ingredients to wet mixture until combined.
5. Roll dough into balls and coat lightly in **powdered sugar.**
6. Bake at **350°F for 10–12 minutes** until cracks form.
7. Cool completely for a "snowy" appearance.

Optional Variations:
- Roll twice in powdered sugar for extra snow effect.
- Add a tiny bit of yellow food coloring for a soft lemon tint.
- Dip cooled cookies in a thin lemon glaze for extra sparkle.

Almond Macaroons

Adapted From: The Rumford Complete Cook Book, 1908

Prep Time: 10 minutes **Bake Time: 15–18 minutes**
Chill Time: None **Servings: 18–24 cookies**

Ingredients

- 1 cup almond paste (or finely ground blanched almonds)
- ½ cup sugar
- 2 egg whites
- ½ tsp almond extract (optional but traditional)
- Pinch of salt

Directions

1. Crumble the **almond paste** into small pieces in a mixing bowl.
2. Add **sugar** and mix with fingers or a fork until combined.
3. Beat the **egg whites** lightly until frothy (not stiff).
4. Add egg whites slowly to the almond mixture—just enough to make a soft, sticky batter.
5. Stir in **almond extract** and a **pinch of salt.**
6. Drop small teaspoonfuls onto a lined baking sheet.
7. Bake at **325°F for 15–18 minutes,** until lightly golden around the edges.
8. Let cool before lifting—they firm up as they stand.

Optional Variations:
- Press a whole almond on top before baking.
- Roll in coarse sugar for sparkle.

Russian Tea Cakes (Snowballs)

Adapted From: Traditional recipes from early 1900s cookbooks

Prep Time: 10 minutes   **Bake Time: 12–14 minutes**
Chill Time: None   **Servings: 24 small cookies**

Ingredients

- 1 cup butter
- ½ cup powdered sugar
- 1 tsp vanilla
- 2¼ cups flour
- ¼ tsp salt
- ¾ cup finely chopped nuts (walnuts or pecans)
- Extra powdered sugar for rolling

Directions

1. Cream **butter and powdered sugar** until smooth.
2. Stir in **vanilla.**
3. Add f**lour, salt, and chopped nuts;** mix until a firm dough forms.
4. Roll dough into small balls.
5. Bake at **350°F for 12–14 minutes,** until bottoms are light golden.
6. While warm, roll cookies in **powdered sugar.**
7. Cool completely and roll again for a snowy finish.

Optional Variations:
- Add a tiny pinch of cinnamon to the dough for warm holiday flavor.

Spice Drop Cookies

Adapted From: The Rumford Complete Cook Book, 1908

Prep Time: 10 minutes
Chill Time: None
Bake Time: 10–12 minutes
Servings: About 24 cookies

Ingredients

- ½ cup butter
- 1 cup brown sugar
- 1 egg
- 2 cups flour
- ½ tsp baking soda

- ½ cup milk
- ½ tsp cinnamon
- ½ tsp nutmeg
- ¼ tsp cloves
- ¼ tsp salt

Optional Powdered Sugar Glaze
- ½ cup powdered sugar
- 1–2 teaspoons milk
- Optional: ⅛ teaspoon vanilla or a pinch of cinnamon

Directions

1. Cream butter and brown sugar.
2. Mix in egg.
3. In a separate bowl, stir together flour, baking soda, salt, and spices.
4. Add dry ingredients to the wet mixture, alternating with milk, until a soft batter forms.
5. Drop spoonfuls of dough onto a baking sheet.
6. Bake at 350°F for 10–12 minutes, until edges are set.

Optional Powdered Sugar Glaze

- **Mix glaze:** Stir powdered sugar with 1 teaspoon milk; add extra drops of milk until smooth and drizzle-ready.
- **Drizzle:** Once cookies are completely cool, drizzle glaze over the tops and let set for 10–15 minutes.

Holiday Vanilla Wafers

Adapted From: The Boston Cooking-School Cook Book, 1896

Prep Time: 10 minutes **Bake Time:** 8–10 minutes
Chill Time: None **Servings:** 24–30 cookies

Ingredients

- ½ cup butter
- 1 cup sugar
- 2 eggs
- 1 tsp vanilla
- 2 cups flour
- ½ tsp baking powder
- ¼ tsp salt
- Optional: red & green holiday sprinkles

Directions

1. Cream **butter and sugar** until light and fluffy.
2. Beat in **eggs and vanilla.**
3. Combine **flour, baking powder, and salt**; stir into the mixture to form a soft dough.
4. Drop small spoonfuls onto a baking sheet.
5. Bake at **350°F for 8–10 minutes,** until edges are lightly golden.

Optional Variations:
- Sprinkle tops with red and green sugar sprinkles before baking for a festive touch.

Orange Spice Cookies

Adapted From: The White House Cook Book, 1887

Prep Time: 10 minutes **Bake Time:** 8-10 minutes
Chill Time: None **Servings:** 24 cookies

Ingredients

- ½ cup butter
- 1 cup sugar
- 1 egg
- Zest of 1 orange
- 1 tbsp orange juice

- 2½ cups flour
- 1 tsp baking powder
- ½ tsp cinnamon
- ¼ tsp nutmeg
- ¼ tsp salt

Orange Glaze (for dipping)
- ½ cup powdered sugar
- 1–2 tbsp orange juice
- ½ tsp orange zest (optional)

Directions

1. Cream **butter and sugar.**
2. Mix in **egg, orange zest, and orange juice.**
3. Stir together **flour, baking powder, salt, cinnamon, and nutmeg.**
4. Add dry ingredients to wet mixture; form a firm dough.
5. Drop by spoonfuls OR roll and cut shapes.
6. Bake at **350°F for 8–10 minutes,** until edges lightly brown.

Optional Orange Glaze (for dipping)
- **Glaze:** Stir ½ cup powdered sugar with 1–2 tbsp orange juice (and ½ tsp zest if desired) until thin.
- **Dip:** Dip the tops of cooled cookies into the glaze, let extra drip off, and place on a rack to dry.

Soft Honey Christmas Cookies

Adapted From: Mrs. Lincoln's Boston Cook Book, 1884

Prep Time: 10 minutes
Chill Time: None

Bake Time: 8-10 minutes
Servings: 24 cookies

Ingredients

- ½ cup honey
- ½ cup sugar
- ½ cup butter
- 1 egg
- 2½ cups flour
- 1 tsp baking powder
- ½ tsp cinnamon
- ¼ tsp ginger
- Pinch of salt

Directions

1. Cream **butter, sugar, and honey** until smooth.
2. Beat in **egg.**
3. In another bowl, combine **flour, baking powder, salt, cinnamon, and ginger.**
4. A dd dry mixture to wet mixture; mix until dough forms.
5. Drop by spoonfuls onto a baking sheet OR roll dough and shape into balls.
6. Bake at **350°F for 8–10 minutes**, until edges are lightly golden.

Optional Variations:
- Add a light drizzle of vanilla icing after cooling for a frosted holiday look.
- Or sprinkle holiday-colored sugar on top before baking.

Chocolate Mint Drop Cookies

Adapted From: The Rumford Complete Cook Book, 1908

Prep Time: 12 minutes
Chill Time: None

Bake Time: 8-10 minutes
Servings: 24 cookies

Ingredients

- ½ cup butter
- 1 cup sugar
- 1 egg
- 1½ cups flour
- ¼ tsp salt

- 2 oz unsweetened chocolate, melted and cooled
- 1 tsp peppermint extract
- ½ tsp baking powder

Mint Glaze (Optional)
- 1 cup powdered sugar
- 1–2 tbsp milk
- ⅛ tsp peppermint extract
- 1–2 drops green food coloring

Directions

1. Cream **butter and sugar u**ntil smooth.
2. Beat in the **egg.**
3. Stir in melted **chocolate and peppermint extract.**
4. In a separate bowl, mix **flour, baking powder, and salt.**
5. Add dry ingredients to the chocolate mixture and stir until fully combined.
6. Drop rounded spoonfuls onto a baking sheet.
7. Bake at **350°F for 8–10 minutes**, until set but still soft.

Optional Mint Glaze
- Let cookies cool completely, then spread a thin layer of the mint glaze on top.
- Drizzle the melted chocolate over the frosted cookies and let set.

Coconut Macaroons

Adapted From: The Neighborhood Cook Book (1912)

Prep Time: 10 minutes
Chill Time: None

Bake Time: 15–18 minutes
Servings: 15–20 cookies

Ingredients

- 2 egg whites
- ½ cup sugar
- 1½–2 cups shredded coconut
- ½ tsp vanilla

Directions

1. Beat the e**gg whites** in a bowl until frothy (not stiff).
2. Stir in the **sugar and vanilla.**
3. Add **shredded coconut**, starting with 1½ cups.
4. Mix until the texture is thick, sticky, and scoopable. Add a little more coconut if the mixture seems too wet.
5. Drop small rounded mounds onto a lined baking sheet.
6. Bake at **325°F for 15–18 minutes,** until the edges turn lightly golden.
7. Cool on the pan until firm enough to lift.

Optional Variations:
- Dip the bottoms in melted chocolate for a fun flavor twist.

Chocolate Snowball Cookies

Adapted From: The Rumford Complete Cook Book, 1908

Prep Time: 10 minutes
Chill Time: 1 hour

Bake Time: 10–12 minutes
Servings: 24 cookies

Ingredients

- 1 cup sugar
- ¼ cup vegetable oil or melted butter
- 2 eggs
- 1 tsp vanilla
- ½ cup unsweetened cocoa powder
- 1 cup flour
- 1 tsp baking powder
- ¼ tsp salt
- Powdered sugar (for rolling)
- Optional: festive chocolate drops

Directions

1. Mix **sugar, oil (or butter), eggs, and vanilla** until smooth.
2. Stir in **cocoa powder.**
3. Add **flour, baking powder, and salt;** mix until a thick dough forms.
4. Chill dough for 1 hour.
5. Roll dough into balls and coat in powdered sugar.
6. Bake at **350°F for 10–12 minutes,** until tops are crackled.

Optional Festive Chocolate Drops

- After baking, gently press a festive chocolate drop into the warm center of each cookie.
- Place cookies in the refrigerator for 30–60 minutes to help the chocolate set.
- Use any decorative festive chocolate drops, such as peppermint-swirl drops or red-and-green confetti drops.

Jam Thumbprint Cookies

Adapted From: Mrs. Lincoln's Boston Cook Book, 1884 (butter cookie base)

Prep Time: 10 minutes   **Bake Time:** 10–12 minutes
Chill Time: None   **Servings:** 20-24 cookies

Ingredients

- ½ cup butter
- ⅓ cup sugar
- 1 egg yolk
- 1 tsp vanilla
- 1¼ cups flour
- Pinch of salt
- Jam or preserves (any flavor: strawberry, raspberry, apricot)

Directions

1. Cream **butter and sugar** until fluffy.
2. Mix in **egg yolk and vanilla.**
3. Stir in **flour and salt** until soft dough forms.
4. Roll dough into small balls (about 1 tablespoon each).
5. Press your thumb gently into the center of each ball to form an indent.
6. Fill each center with **jam** (½ to 1 teaspoon).
7. Bake at **350°F for 10–12 minutes,** until edges are lightly golden.
8. Cool completely before stacking or storing.

Optional Variations:
- Use two jam flavors side-by-side for a "candy swirl" look.

(Example: strawberry + lemon, raspberry + apricot.)

Spritz Butter Cookies

Adapted From: The Settlement Cookbook, 1901

Prep Time: 10 minutes
Chill Time: None

Bake Time: 7–9 minutes
Servings: 30–40 small cookies

Ingredients

- 1 cup butter
- ¾ cup sugar
- 1 egg
- 1 tsp vanilla or almond extract
- 2¼ cups flour
- ¼ tsp salt
- Optional: holiday sprinkles or colored sugars

Directions

1. Cream **butter and sugar** until light and fluffy.
2. Add e**gg and vanilla (or almond extract)** and mix well.
3. Stir in f**lour and salt** until a soft dough forms.
4. Load dough into a cookie press.
5. Press cookies directly onto an ungreased sheet in any shape you like— trees, stars, wreaths, flowers.
6. Add sprinkles if desired.
7. Bake at **375°F for 7–9 minutes,** until edges are lightly golden.

Optional Decorating Ideas:
- Use green sprinkles for trees
- Use red and white sugars for wreaths
- Add a single chocolate dot or candy in the center of the flower shapes

Oatmeal Raisin Spice Cookies

Adapted From: The Rumford Complete Cook Book, 1908

Prep Time: 10 minutes

Chill Time: None

Bake Time: 10–12 minutes

Servings: 24 cookies

Ingredients

- ½ cup butter
- ¾ cup brown sugar
- 1 egg
- 1 tsp vanilla
- ¾ cup flour
- ½ tsp baking soda
- ¼ tsp salt
- 1 tsp cinnamon
- ¼ tsp nutmeg
- 1½ cups rolled oats
- ½ cup raisins (optional: substitute dried cranberries)

Directions

1. Cream **butter and brown sugar** until smooth.
2. Beat in **egg and vanilla**.
3. Stir together **flour, baking soda, salt, cinnamon, and nutmeg.**
4. Add dry mixture to the wet mixture.
5. Fold in **oats and raisins**.
6. Drop spoonfuls onto a cookie sheet.
7. Bake at **350°F for 10–12 minutes,** until edges are golden.

Optional Variations:

- Add 2 tbsp mini chocolate chips for extra sweetness
- Swap raisins for dried cranberries for a Christmas red color

Raisin Nut Cookies

Adapted From: The White House Cook Book (1887)

Prep Time: 10 minutes
Chill Time: None

Bake Time: 10–12 minutes
Servings: 20-24 cookies

Ingredients

- ½ cup butter
- 1 cup sugar
- 1 egg
- 1 tsp vanilla
- 1¾ cups flour

- 1 tsp baking powder
- ¼ tsp salt
- ½ tsp cinnamon
- ½ cup chopped nuts (walnuts or pecans)
- ½ cup raisins

Directions

1. Cream butter and sugar together until smooth and fluffy.
2. Add the egg and vanilla; mix until combined.
3. In a separate bowl, whisk together flour, baking powder, salt, and cinnamon.
4. Stir dry ingredients into the butter mixture.
5. Add raisins and chopped nuts; mix until evenly combined.
6. Drop rounded spoonfuls onto a baking sheet, leaving space between each.
7. Bake at 350°F for 10–12 minutes, or until lightly golden on the edges.

Optional Variations:
- Gently press one extra raisin or nut on top of each cookie before baking, for decoration.

46

Candy Cane Twist Cookies

Adapted From: The Boston Cooking-School Cook Book (1896)

Prep Time: 15 minutes
Chill Time: None

Bake Time: 8-10 minutes
Servings: 20-24 cookies

Ingredients

- ½ cup butter
- ½ cup sugar
- 1 egg
- 1 tsp vanilla
- 1½ cups flour

- ½ tsp baking powder
- ¼ tsp salt
- Red food coloring (gel preferred)

Directions

1. Cream the **butter and sugar** together until light and fluffy.
2. Beat in the **egg and vanilla.**
3. In a separate bowl, whisk the **flour, baking powder, and salt**.
4. Add dry ingredients to the butter mixture and stir until a soft dough forms.
5. Divide the dough in half.
6. Leave one half plain; knead **red food coloring** into the other half.
7. Roll a small piece of each color into **thin ropes**.
8. Twist one red rope and one plain rope together to form a candy cane shape.
9. Gently curve the top into the cane hook.
10. Place onto a baking sheet.
11. Bake at **350°F for 8–10** minutes, until set but not browned.

48

Ginger Molasses Drop Cookies

Adapted From: Mrs. Lincoln's Boston Cook Book (1884)

Prep Time: 10 minutes **Bake Time:** 10–12 minutes
Chill Time: None **Servings:** 20-24 cookies

Ingredients

- ½ cup butter (softened)
- ½ cup sugar
- ½ cup molasses
- 1 egg
- 2 cups flour
- 1 tsp baking soda
- ½ tsp cinnamon
- ½ tsp ginger
- ¼ tsp cloves
- ¼ tsp salt

Directions

1. Cream together the softened **butter and sugar** until smooth.
2. Stir in the **egg and molasses** until fully combined.
3. In a separate bowl, whisk the f**lour, baking soda, salt, cinnamon, ginger, and cloves**.
4. Add dry ingredients to the wet mixture and stir until a soft dough forms.
5. Drop rounded spoonfuls of dough onto a baking sheet.
6. Bake at **350°F for 10–12 minutes,** until the edges are lightly set and tops crackle softly.

Optional Variations:
- Roll the dough balls lightly in sugar before baking for a sweet sparkle.
- For extra "snow-dusted" cookies, sprinkle a touch of powdered sugar on warm cookies after baking.

50

Christmas Cut-Out Sugar Cookies

Adapted From: The Boston Cooking-School Cook Book (1896)

Prep Time: 15 minutes   **Bake Time:** 8-10 minutes
Chill Time: 30 minutes   **Servings:** 24-30 cookies

Ingredients

- ½ cup butter
- 1 cup sugar
- 1 egg
- 1 tsp vanilla
- 2 cups flour
- 1½ tsp baking powder
- ¼ tsp salt
- 2–3 tbsp milk (as needed for soft dough)

Directions

1. In a large bowl, cream the **butter and sugar** until light and fluffy.
2. Beat in the **egg and vanilla** until smooth.
3. In a separate bowl, whisk together **flour, baking powder, and salt.**
4. Add the dry mixture to the butter mixture.
5. Add **milk a little at a time** until the dough becomes soft and workable.
6. Flatten dough into a disk, wrap, and chill for 30 minutes for easier cutting.
7. Roll out chilled dough on a floured surface to about ¼-inch thickness.
8. Use cookie cutters to cut out holiday shapes: trees, stars, ornaments, snowflakes, etc.
9. Place shapes onto a baking sheet.
10. Bake at **350°F for 8–10 minutes,** until the edges are just barely golden.
11. **Optional:** Decorate with colored sugar before baking for a classic old-fashioned sparkle.

✨ Santa & Reindeer Extra Treats ✨

🎅 Santa's Treats
- Santa's Hot Chocolate
- Santa's Favorite Chocolate Chip Cookies

🎄 Holiday Kid Favorites
- Gumdrop Cookies

🦌 Reindeer Treats
- ⭐ Magic Reindeer Food
- ⭐ Reindeer Carrot Snacks

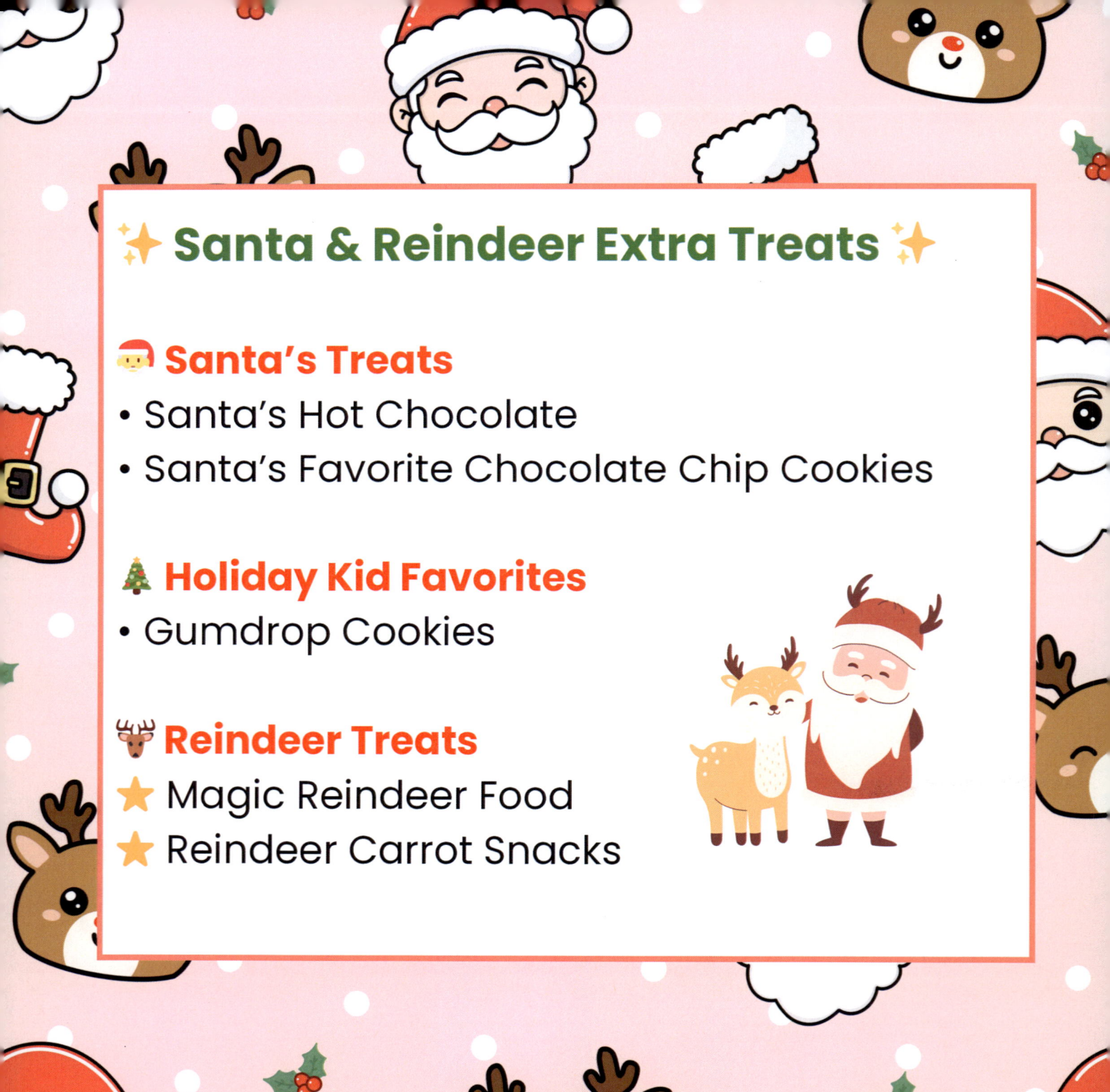

Santa's Hot Chocolate

Adapted From: Adapted from classic early 1900s hot cocoa methods

Prep Time: 5 minutes **Servings:** 2 mugs
Cook Time: 5 minutes

Ingredients

- 2 cups milk
- 2 tbsp unsweetened cocoa powder
- 2 tbsp sugar
- ¼ tsp vanilla
- Pinch of salt
- Marshmallows (optional)

Directions

1. In a small pot, whisk the **cocoa powder, sugar, and salt** together.
2. Add **2–3 tablespoons of milk** and stir until smooth like chocolate syrup.
3. Pour in the **rest of the milk** and heat over medium, stirring gently.
4. Warm until hot (but do not boil).
5. Remove from heat and stir in **vanilla.**
6. Pour into mugs.

Optional Variations:
- Add mini marshmallows on top.
- Sprinkle a little cinnamon or crushed peppermint for a holiday twist.

Santa's Favorite Chocolate Chip Cookies

Adapted From: The Rumford Complete Cook Book, 1908

Prep Time: 10 minutes
Chill Time: None

Bake Time: 8-10 minutes
Servings: 24 cookies

Ingredients

- ½ cup butter (softened)
- ½ cup sugar
- ½ cup brown sugar
- 1 egg
- 1 tsp vanilla
- 1⅓ cups flour
- ½ tsp baking soda
- ¼ tsp salt
- 1 cup chocolate chips

Directions

1. Cream together the softened **butter, white sugar, and brown sugar** until fluffy.
2. Beat in the **egg and vanilla.**
3. In a separate bowl, mix the **flour, baking soda, and salt**.
4. Stir the dry mixture into the butter mixture until combined.
5. Fold in the **chocolate chips.**
6. Drop rounded spoonfuls of dough onto a baking sheet.
7. Bake at **350°F for 8–10 minutes,** until edges are set and centers look soft.
8. Cool on the pan for a couple minutes, then move to a rack.

Optional Variations:
- Add festive red & green sprinkles before baking for a holiday look.

Gumdrop Cookies (Holiday Kid Favorite)

Adapted From: early 1900s public-domain fruit drop cookie formulas

Prep Time: 10 minutes
Chill Time: None

Bake Time: 10–12 minutes
Servings: 20-24 cookies

Ingredients

- ½ cup butter
- 1 cup sugar
- 1 egg
- 1 tsp vanilla
- 2 cups flour
- ½ tsp baking soda
- ¼ tsp salt
- ½ cup finely chopped fruit-flavored gumdrops

(Use firm gumdrops, not spice drops; avoid black licorice pieces.)

Directions

1. Cream the **butter and sugar** together until fluffy.
2. Beat in the **egg and vanilla**.
3. In a separate bowl, whisk together **flour, baking soda, and salt**.
4. Stir dry mixture into the **butter mixture**.
5. Add the **chopped gumdrops** and gently fold them in.
6. Drop rounded spoonfuls of dough onto a baking sheet.
7. Bake at **350°F for 10–12 minutes**, until edges are golden and centers are set.

Optional Variations:

- Use red, green, and white gumdrops for extra Christmas colors.
- Press one tiny gumdrop piece on top of each cookie before baking for a colorful "jewel" effect.

Magic Reindeer Food

Adapted From: A classic holiday tradition

Prep Time: 10 minutes
Chill Time: None

Bake Time: 10–12 minutes
Servings: 24 cookies

Ingredients

- ½ cup rolled oats
- 2 tbsp red or green sugar sprinkles
- 1 tbsp sparkling sugar or coarse sugar
- Pinch of cinnamon (optional)

Directions

1. Stir the oats, sprinkles, sugar, and cinnamon together in a small bowl.
2. Pour the mixture into a small pouch or cup.
3. On Christmas Eve, sprinkle the Magic Reindeer Food outside so Santa's team can find your home!

Reindeer Carrot Snacks

Adapted From: A classic holiday tradition

Prep Time: 5 minutes **Bake Time:** NA
Chill Time: None **Servings:** 8–10 small treats

Ingredients

- 2 large carrots
- 2 tbsp honey or maple syrup
- 1 tbsp water
- ¼ tsp cinnamon (optional)

Directions

1. Peel and slice the **carrots** into sticks or small coins.
2. Stir the **honey and water** together.
3. Drizzle lightly over the carrots and toss to coat.
4. Add a **pinch of cinnamon** if desired.
5. Set them out for Santa's reindeer to enjoy!

Bonus Printable Coloring Pages

Enjoy printable 8.5 × 11 versions of the bonus coloring pages—easy to print at home, and you may print them as many times as you'd like. These pages are for personal use only and may not be shared, resold, uploaded, or distributed.

To download and print the Bonus Coloring pages, Scan the QR code or visit: https://is.gd/6tY7rP

We'd Love Your Feedback

Thank you for reading. Please consider leaving a review on Amazon. Your feedback helps others discover the book and supports future recipes!